SATURN

MONIQUE VESCIA

Britannica
Educational Publishing
IN ASSOCIATION

ROSEN
EDUCATIONAL SERVICES

Published in 2017 by Britannica Educational Publishing (a trademark of Encyclopædia Britannica, Inc.) in association with The Rosen Publishing Group, Inc.
29 East 21st Street, New York, NY 10010

Distributed exclusively by Rosen Publishing.
To see additional Britannica Educational Publishing titles, go to rosenpublishing.com.

First Edition

Britannica Educational Publishing
J.E. Luebering: Executive Director, Core Editorial
Mary Rose McCudden: Editor, Britannica Student Encyclopedia

Rosen Publishing
Nicholas Croce: Editor
Nelson Sá: Art Director
Michael Moy: Designer
Cindy Reiman: Photography Manager
Bruce Donnola: Photo Researcher

Library of Congress Cataloging-in-Publication Data

Names: Vescia, Monique.
Title: Saturn / Monique Vescia.
Description: First edition. | New York : Britannica Educational Publishing in association with Rosen Educational Services, 2017. | Series: Planetary exploration | Includes bibliographical references and index.
Identifiers: LCCN 2016020481 | ISBN 9781508104179 (library bound) | ISBN 9781508104186 (pbk.) | ISBN 9781508103080 (6-pack)
Subjects: LCSH: Saturn (Planet)—Juvenile literature. | Solar system—Juvenile literature.
Classification: LCC QB671 .V47 2017 | DDC 523.46—dc23
LC record available at https://lccn.loc.gov/2016020481

Manufactured in China

Photo credits: Cover MarcelClemens/Shutterstock.com (Saturn); cover and interior pages background Jurik Peter/Shutterstock.com; pp. 4, 9, 16, 26, 28 NASA/JPL/Space Science Institute; p. 5 Roberto Zilli/Shutterstock.com; p. 6 NASA/Lunar and Planetary Laboratory; p. 7 NASA/JPL/Caltech (NASA photo # PIA00024); p. 8 Encyclopædia Britannica, Inc.; p. 10, 17 NASA/JPL-Caltech/Space Science Institute; p. 11 © NASA/SSPL/The Image Works; p. 12 Space Frontiers/Archive Photos/Getty Images; pp. 13, 14, 23 NASA/JPL; p. 15 ESA/NASA/JPL/University of Arizona; p. 18 Mark Garlick/Science Source; p. 19 Roger Harris/Science Source; p. 20 Detlev van Ravenswaay/Science Source; p. 21 Julian Baum/Science Source; p. 22 Hulton Archive/Getty Images; pp. 24, 29 NASA; p. 25 Science & Society Picture Library/Getty Images; p. 27 Science Source.

CONTENTS

JEWEL OF THE SOLAR SYSTEM

Many people consider Saturn the most beautiful planet of all. Its wonderful rings and golden color have earned it the nickname "Jewel of the Solar System."

Saturn is a favorite planet of **astronomers**. Even a small telescope can be used to view the planet's beautiful rings. Without a telescope, Saturn looks like a bright point of light in the night sky. This is how it appeared to ancient astronomers.

Advances in technology can now bring us vivid images of the beautiful planet that has fascinated humans for ages.

Thousands of years ago, astronomers observed lights in the night sky and named them after their gods and goddesses. Saturn gets its name from the ancient Roman god of agriculture.

Today, people know far more about Saturn than was known in ancient times. Unmanned spacecraft send back incredible images that add to our understanding. Still, this mysterious and lovely planet continues to fascinate us.

The ancient Romans built temples to the gods and godesses they worshipped. This one is dedicated to Saturn.

SIXTH FROM THE SUN

The closest that Saturn and Earth will ever get to each other is about 746 million miles (1.2 billion kilometers). In the solar system, Saturn is the sixth planet from the sun. (Earth is the third from the sun.) Saturn's orbit is between that of Jupiter and Uranus.

This illustration shows the order of the planets and also includes the dwarf planet Pluto. Saturn, with its distinct rings, is sixth from the sun.

In what way is Saturn similar to Earth? How is it different, and why?

Saturn belongs to the group of outer planets. The other outer planets are Jupiter, Uranus, and Neptune. These four planets are less dense than the rocky inner planets that are closer to the sun. They are also much larger.

Saturn is a cold planet even though it is a warm golden color. Its average temperature is −288° F (−178° C). Unlike on Earth, temperatures vary only a little between the planet's equator and its poles.

All of the outer planets in the solar system have rings, but Saturn's are the most spectacular.

SIZING UP SATURN

Saturn is the second largest planet in the solar system. Its **diameter** is 74,900 miles (120,600 km). That is more than nine times longer than the diameter of Earth. Saturn is about 95 times as massive as Earth.

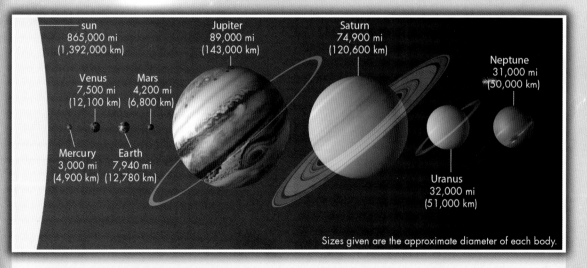

sun
865,000 mi
(1,392,000 km)

Venus
7,500 mi
(12,100 km)

Mars
4,200 mi
(6,800 km)

Mercury
3,000 mi
(4,900 km)

Earth
7,940 mi
(12,780 km)

Jupiter
89,000 mi
(143,000 km)

Saturn
74,900 mi
(120,600 km)

Neptune
31,000 mi
(50,000 km)

Uranus
32,000 mi
(51,000 km)

Sizes given are the approximate diameter of each body.

Saturn is much larger than any of the other planets in the solar system—except for Jupiter.

Diameter is the measurement of a straight line passing from side to side through the middle of a circle or a sphere.

Saturn's nearest neighbor is Jupiter. It is most similar to that planet in size and composition. Like Jupiter, Saturn is made up mostly of gases. Beneath an outer layer of gases is a smaller area of hot liquid metal. Saturn's center is likely a hot core of rock.

Saturn usually appears to have a yellowish-brown color. Scientists believe this color is due to chemicals in the planet's clouds. Cloudless areas are often blue. These colors shift on the planet at different times during its path around the sun.

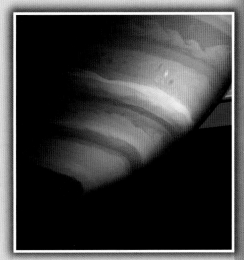

False-color photos of Saturn make it easier to see the planet's clouds.

A PLANET THAT CAN FLOAT

Like all of the outer planets in the solar system, Saturn is a gas giant. It is made up of a mixture of gases. This makes landing a vehicle for exploration on Saturn impossible, as there is no solid surface on which to land.

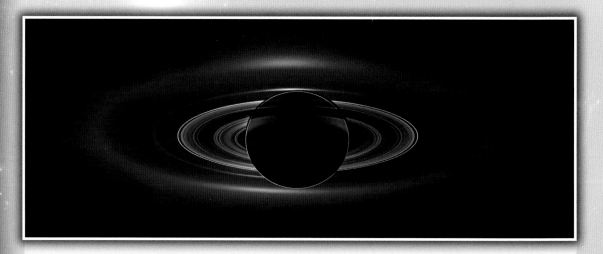

Saturn is made up of mostly hydrogen. Hydrogen is the lightest chemical element.

THINK ABOUT IT

No bathtub is big enough for Saturn to fit in, so how do you think scientists can determine that Saturn is less dense than water and would float in it?

Scientists think that 73 to 80 percent of Saturn is made of hydrogen. The remaining portion is mostly helium. In some parts of the planet these chemicals are in liquid form.

Of all the planets in the solar system, Saturn is the least dense, or compact. It is less dense than water. In comparison, Jupiter is a bit denser than water, and Earth is about five times denser than water. In a bathtub of water as big as the universe, Saturn would float!

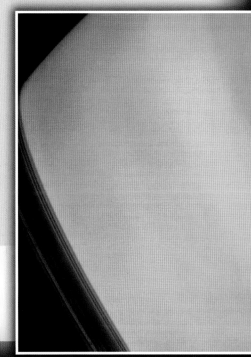

Saturn would swallow any spacecraft that tried to land on it because it has no surface on which to land.

RINGS OF ICE

Saturn's most amazing feature is its rings. The other outer planets also have rings but they are thinner and less bright than the rings of Saturn.

Saturn's hundreds of thousands of thin rings are made up of particles of ice and dust. These particles can be as large as a house or even as small as a speck of dust.

Saturn's widest rings occur in groups that scientists have named after letters in the alphabet, from A to G. Saturn's narrower rings have been given other names. The

Astronomers today have a good understanding of the makeup and origin of Saturn's rings.

When Saturn spins and moves around the sun, what keeps its rings from drifting away from the planet into space?

D ring is closest to the planet, followed by the C ring and B ring. Four narrow rings, or ringlets, exist between rings C and B. Beyond that extends another ringlet, several gaps, and nine more rings. The farthest ring reaches about 8 million miles (12.8 million km) away from Saturn into space. The gaps between the rings are named for astronomers.

This view of Saturn's rings was taken by the Cassini spacecraft in 2005.

MANY MOONS

Astronomers have identified more than sixty moons that orbit Saturn. The planet's eight large inner moons are thought to have formed along with Saturn about 4.6 billion years ago. They orbit in nearly circular paths at or near the same level as Saturn's path around the sun. Saturn's outer moons, however, follow long or tilted orbits around the planet.

Saturn's largest moon is Titan. It is the second largest moon in the solar system after Jupiter's moon Ganymede. Unlike any other moon in the solar system, Titan has clouds and an atmo-

Ganymede is brownish-gray. Recent impact craters show up as bright spots on the moon's surface.

sphere. Its atmosphere is even denser, or thicker, than Earth's atmosphere.

Several smaller moons are in Saturn's rings. The gravity of these moons affects the particles in the rings. The moons may clear away particles from their own orbit and create gaps in the ring system. Some of the moons keep material in place within a ring. The moons Pandora and Prometheus orbit on either side of the F ring. They force its particles into a narrow band.

Scientists believe that what appear to be stones on Titan's surface may actually be frozen clumps of water ice.

Saturn has an enormous **atmosphere**. It is mostly made up of hydrogen, with some helium and even smaller amounts of other gases. Saturn may look beautiful from afar but the planet's weather is terrible. Imagine a hurricane with winds nearly 1,100 miles (1,800 km) per hour. That's about seven times faster than the fastest winds on Earth!

Saturn's strongest winds blow across the planet's equator in the same direction as the planet's rotation, eastward.

Bands of clouds whip across Saturn's surface, seen here in black and white, in the planet's southern hemisphere.

The mass of gases that surrounds a planet is called its atmosphere.

Westward winds move much more slowly. Saturn's winds push the clouds. The clouds appear as stripes that surround the planet. As on Jupiter, giant storm systems appear on Saturn as brown, white, and red ovals. A very large storm occurs on Saturn every thirty years, or about once every orbit. In addition, two huge, permanent cyclones exist at the planet's north and south poles.

A unique cloud pattern shaped as a hexagon constantly appears at Saturn's north pole, where it surrounds a fixed cyclone.

BENEATH THE SURFACE

The temperature and pressure are very high inside Saturn, and they increase with depth. No living creature could survive such pressure. Hydrogen gas inside Saturn is squeezed until it turns into liquid. The dense core of the planet is probably a mixture of rock, metal, and some gases. Scientists think this core is ten to twenty times the mass of Earth.

Saturn gives off twice as much energy as it receives from the

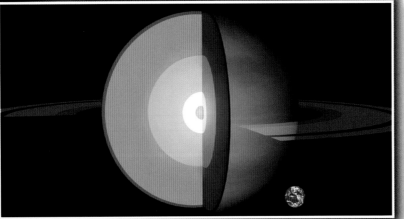

This illustration shows what Saturn's interior—made up of gas, liquid, and rock—may look like.

Do you think that scientists will change their ideas about Saturn's inside as new information becomes available to them?

sun, mostly as heat. This means that the planet produces some of its own heat. This energy is probably left over from when the planet formed about 4.6 billion years ago. Since then Saturn has slowly cooled down and gradually released heat.

Saturn's gravity is stronger at the north and south poles than at the equator. Studying Saturn's gravity field has helped scientists learn more about what is inside the planet.

To reach Saturn, energy from the sun travels about 9.5 times farther than it does to reach Earth.

SPINNING AROUND THE SUN

L ike all planets, Saturn has two types of motion: orbit and spin. Saturn revolves around the sun in an **elliptical** orbit. It takes about twenty-nine Earth years for the planet to make one complete trip around the sun.

Saturn's day lasts only eleven hours because the planet spins very quickly. Saturn is mostly made up of layers of gases, so parts of the

A year on Saturn lasts much longer than a year on Earth because it is so far from the sun.

planet spin at different speeds. Though all parts of the planet spin quickly, the clouds at Saturn's equator spin fastest.

Saturn is tilted on its axis as it orbits the sun. The axis is an imaginary line that runs through a planet's center from pole to pole. Saturn's tilted axis causes its rings to appear at different angles to viewers on Earth. Saturn's tilted axis also causes the planet to experience seasons as it orbits the sun. Each season on Saturn lasts more than seven Earth years.

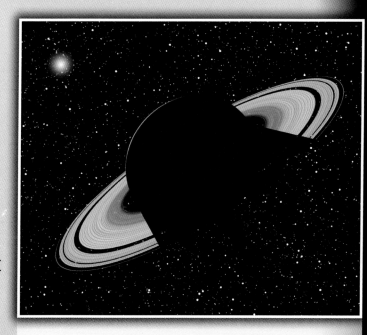

Saturn's tilted axis allows us to see its extraordinary rings.

EARLY OBSERVATIONS

Saturn is called a "naked-eye planet" because it can be seen without using a telescope. Ancient astronomers were able to see Saturn, as well as the other naked-eye planets: Mercury, Venus, Mars, and Jupiter.

In 1610 Italian astronomer Galileo Galilei viewed Saturn through an early telescope. At first he thought he was seeing a group of three stars. Later he thought he saw one object with strange

Galileo used these telescopes to study Saturn and other bodies in the night sky. Today's powerful telescopes can peer much farther into space.

By the early 1600s several people had made simple telescopes. How do you think people studied and learned about the solar system before the invention of the telescope?

shapes on either side of it that he described as ears. He never realized the strange shapes were Saturn's rings.

In 1655 Dutch astronomer Christiaan Huygens used a stronger telescope and saw ring shapes around the planet. Huygens thought that the rings were solid, flat disks. Centuries later, scientists proved that Saturn's rings cannot be solid and must be made up of many small particles.

Centuries after Galileo first viewed Saturn through a telescope, the Cassini–Huygens spacecraft traveled to Saturn to study it up close.

UNMANNED MISSIONS

The first spacecraft to reach Saturn was named Pioneer 11. This unmanned craft was launched by the U.S. National Aeronautics and Space Administration (NASA). In September 1979 it flew within 13,000 miles (21,000 km) of the planet's atmosphere. The photographs and data that Pioneer 11 sent back to Earth allowed scientists to identify previously unknown moons and the planet's F ring.

In November 1980, the Voyager 1 spacecraft captured this image of Dione, one of Saturn's many moons.

Many popular science fiction television shows and movies feature outer space exploration. How do real space missions differ from fictional ones?

NASA sent two more unmanned spacecraft to Saturn. Voyager 1 reached the planet in November 1980 and Voyager 2 arrived in August 1981. The Voyager spacecraft sent back tens of thousands of images. From these, scientists could see that Saturn's rings have a very complex structure. Scientists also learned of previously unknown moons among the planet's rings.

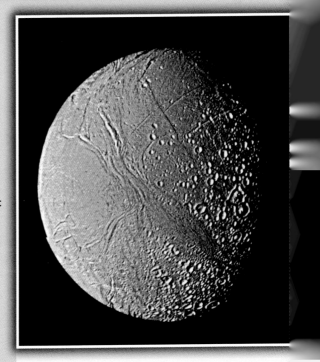

Voyager 2 took this image of Enceladus, one of Saturn's moons. The surface grooves may be a sign of volcanic activity.

PROBING FOR ANSWERS

The moon Dione is shown here in its orbit around Saturn. The thin line below it is a side view of Saturn's rings.

The Cassini-Huygens mission to study Saturn was launched in 1997. It consisted of NASA's Cassini orbiter and the European Space Agency's Huygens probe. Cassini-Huygens began orbiting Saturn in July 2004. Five months later the Huygens probe was released toward Saturn's largest moon, Titan.

Several weeks later the Huygens probe landed on Titan. During its descent, the probe took 350 photographs of the moon's features, including a shoreline and the mouth of a river. Huygens was the first spacecraft to land on a body in space beyond Mars.

Cassini sent back data about six new moons and two new rings of Saturn. The orbiter also identified ice geysers on the moon Enceladus, and large lakes of liquid methane on Titan. Scientists expect that after a close encounter with Titan, Cassini will end its mission by falling out of orbit and into Saturn.

Backlit by the sun's rays, geysers spew water vapor and ice from Enceladus's frosty surface.

A CLOSER LOOK

There is much more to learn about Saturn. A joint mission between the United States and Europe is planned to launch from Earth in 2020. One goal of the mission is to return to Saturn's cloud-covered moon, Titan. Scientists think Titan may be similar to a young Earth before much life existed on Earth's surface. The moon Enceladus is another target of the mission. Scientists want to find out if there is a source of water for that moon's geysers.

This view of Titan was taken by the Cassini spacecraft. Bright methane clouds appear at the bottom of the photograph near the moon's south pole.

Another exciting idea for future exploration is to send a submarine to explore Kraken Mare, Titan's largest northern sea. The submarine would travel beneath the surface and transmit its findings back to Earth.

Who knows what future missions to Saturn will discover? One thing is sure: This beautiful planet and its marvelous rings will always continue to amaze us.

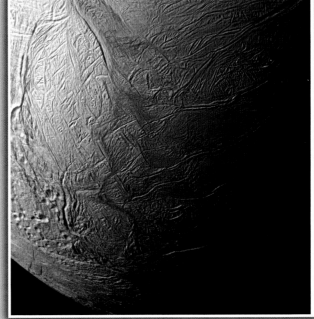

Scientists are interested in Enceladus because there is evidence that the moon has liquid water.

GLOSSARY

AXIS An imaginary line through the middle of an object, around which that object spins.

DENSITY A measure of how much of an object's material is in a given space or how compact the object is.

ENERGY Usable power or the ability to do work that comes in many forms, such as heat, electricity, and sunlight.

EQUATOR An imaginary circle around a planet that is always the same distance from the north pole and the south pole.

GEYSER A hole in the ground that shoots out hot water and steam.

GRAVITY A pulling force between any two objects that works across space.

HELIUM The second-most common chemical element in the universe. It is usually a gas.

HEXAGON A six-sided shape.

HYDROGEN The most common chemical element in the universe. It is usually a gas.

MASS The amount of physical matter that an object contains.

METHANE A colorless odorless flammable gas that consists of carbon and hydrogen.

MISSION A flight by an aircraft or spacecraft to perform a specific task.

MOON A satellite of a planet.

ORBIT The path taken by one body circling around another body.

PRESSURE The application of force exerted on something by something else in direct contact with it.

RADIATE To give off energy in the form of rays.

SPACECRAFT A vehicle for travel beyond Earth's atmosphere.

TELESCOPE A device that uses lenses, or curved mirrors and lenses, to make distant objects look closer and larger.

TRANSMIT To send a signal by radio waves.

UNMANNED Having no person aboard.

FOR MORE INFORMATION

Books

Bloom, J. P. *Saturn*. Minneapolis, MN: Abdo Kids, 2015.

DiSiena, Laura Lyn, and Hannah Eliot. *Saturn Could Sail: and Other Fun Facts*. New York, NY: Little Simon, 2014.

Glaser, Chaya. *Saturn: Amazing Rings*. New York, NY: Bearport Publishing, 2015.

Nichols, Amie. *Journey to Saturn*. New York, NY: PowerKids Press, 2015.

Owen, Ruth. *Saturn*. New York, NY: Windmill Books, 2014.

Radomski, Kassandra. *The Secrets of Saturn*. North Mankato, MN: Capstone Press, 2016.

Roumanis, Alexis. *Saturn*. New York, NY: AV2 by Weigl, 2016.

Squire, Ann. *Planet Saturn*. New York, NY: Children's Press, 2014.

Websites

Because of the changing nature of internet links, Rosen Publishing has developed an online list of websites related to the subject of this book. This site is updated regularly. Please use this link to access the list:

http://www.rosenlinks.com/PE/saturn

INDEX